STILL WATER –

A COLLECTION

Other Books by Don Davison

An Outline of a Philosophy of the Consciousness of Truth
The Concept of Personhood in the Evolutionary Process of Being
The Game of Life: A Player's Manual for Executives and Others
Sign Posts: A Collection of Essays, Volumes I, II, III, IV, and V

Poetry

Thoughts and Feelings Book I
Thoughts and Feelings Book II
Needles from the Ponderosas at Zirahuen
Seeds from the Ponderosas at Zirahuen
Pitch from the Ponderosas at Zirahuen
Humus from the Ponderosas at Zirahuen
Sawdust from the Ponderosas at Zirahuen
Sun's Rays Bouncing off the Ponderosas at Zirahuen
Shadows Beneath the Ponderosas at Zirahuen
Cones from the Ponderosas at Zirahuen
Pollen Sifting from the Ponderosas at Zirahuen
Reflections from Lucerne
Searching Swamps
Questions
Time's Echoes
Memories
Insistences
Splashes
Ripples
Pebbles

Collections

Always Extolling
Murmurings
Iris and Other Things
Pieces of the Journey
Reflections from Lucerne
The Twelfth Hour
Pebbles on the Shore
Through the Swamps of Time

STILL WATER –

A COLLECTION

Don Davison

Published by Zirahuen

Published by Zirahuen
P.O. Box 30933
Flagstaff, AZ 84003
pathtotheself.com
DrDavison@pathtotheself.com

©2015 by Zirahuen
All rights reserved. Published 2015
Printed in the United States of America

ISBN 978-0-9858130-4-8

No part of this book may be used or reproduced in any manner whatsoever without written permission, except in the case of brief quotations embodied in critical articles and review.

Cover photo is Pondevron at Timber Ranch
Author photo by Patricia Davison

Special thanks to Louella Holter, and to Tina Rosio, from W.

Again –
To Patricia, for everything.

All of Don Davison's books have water on their covers. Water is one of the most essential attributes of the planet Earth; without it, life as we know it would not exist. It deserves our most considered attention.

Davison's collections of poetry all end with "Finding Pieces." Many of you have asked, where did the rules for the Game of Life come from? They come from many places and different times. Good hunting!

CONTENTS

Wisdom from the Old Pueblo	1
Be Aware!	2
Anchored Remembering	3
Humankind	4
Some Statements	5
The Other Side	6
To Dream the Dream	7
Clutching Hands	8
We Act In Ways	9
Raven's Dance	10
Sandals – No More	11
To Be One – We Must Be Two	12
Empty Tree	13
Idiomatic Revelance	14
Necessary Things	15
Hands On!	16
Pinheads	17
The Masses	18
Awe Struck	19
Beheld	20
It Has Been Said	21
Messianic Hubris	22
A Vision	23
To Motivate a Few	24
Cheating Time	25
Gifts	26
Lost and Found	27
Our Time	28

Self-Respect	29
The Axe Strikes the Tree	30
Yes and No	31
Obuntu	32
History	33
The Last Conflagration	34
Choices	35
On My Way Again	36
The Voice of the People	37
The Question	39
A Statement of Fact	40
A Vast Panorama	41
A Modern Disease	42
Another Realization	43
Scratchings	44
An Age Upon Us	45
Conundrum	47
Assessment	48
Death's Words	49
Discrimination	50
Admonition	51
A Wish	52
Facts	53
Facts or Fiction?	54
From Whence the Prophets?	55
Impassioned	56
Jihad	57
Land	58
Post-It Note	59
Selling the Land	60
Sleep	61
Still Blinded	62
A Description of Confusion	63
Wrong Choice	64
Winning the Prize	65

What's He Doing?	66
We Are All Children	67
Truth's Ladder	68
The Lie	69
Tragic-Comedy	70
The Idiocy of It All	71
Grand Design	73
The Double-Edge Sword	74
Age Wears	76
What Am I Doing?	77
Almost …	78
Drowning	79
Just A Few	80
Left To Tell (And Found)	81
Pay Attention Or Die!	82
The Dying and the Dead	83
The Orb	84
The Soul Speaks	85
Dawn Rises	86
My Father and My Brother – And All His Friends Too!	87
Sedona Moment	89
To the Post-Postmoderns	90
The Age's Wisdom	91
To the Bastards of Dead Creek	92
The Floundering Footsteps of History	94
I Cannot Go – I Cannot Stay	95
Every Life	96
The All of History	97
Fleeting Thoughts	99
Found	100
Exit Stage Left	101
Another Question – Another Answer	103
A Person	104
Our Greatest Lie	106

Who's Nature?	107
We Plant Stones	108
A Resting Place: For All the Old Loggers	109
Nu-Roc	121

WISDOM FROM THE OLD PUEBLO

"Tell me,
What good's your life?"
"It must be to know another to love."
"Does that just mean more conundrums?"

BE AWARE!

When is our life an easy set of circumstances?
When the silent whirlpool eases off
into a calm stream
and we float and wonder what caught us
and held us for that brief moment.
It is in our recollection that we are caught and loosened
and caught and loosened again.
By whom do the vagaries of time
sway back and forth?
It has been written,
"We know so little and pretend so much."[1]
Of a time we all come to know,
"*We* must ride, always aware, and always ready."

---

[1] From "Species Lost" in *Through the Swamps of Time: A Collection*.

ANCHORED REMEMBERING

I am
a pushed pulled
synaptic archipelago
mirroring a fast slow.

HUMANKIND

Does the sunrise care,
or the moonrise concern itself,
or the gentle rains
that wash the rocks and dampen the soil
languish in despair?
Do they know who hates and who loves?
Is their charge to bless each and every thing
according to its kind?
If this is so then why do Islamists kill their own,
and Protestants Catholics and
Arabs Jews and
Jews Arabs,
and neighbors neighbors,
and husbands wives,
and sisters brothers,
and nations others?
Where do I seek the answers to my questions?
A voice whispers,
"In the depths and breadths
of the heart
of humankind."

SOME STATEMENTS

A metaphor for human life is the making of a "now"
that becomes a whole –
like a layering of the Toledo swords,
so desired in those moments of the past.
How is it that the sacred aspect of dialog has been lost
(or apparently lost)
just when we need it so much?
A stalemate is not a part of nature's way.
The edges of the difference will clash
and that may not be in the best interests
of the parts or of the whole.
Everything is:
Food for thought apprehended in word
leading to action.
Life is thoughtful doing,
a conversation with action.
And still people get sanctimonious
about being wrong.
Soul is an innate purposefulness
that has direction.
For the solace of the other,
I offer all that I do.
We live wanting to be
"more than a self."
Then,
we realize a self is always a self in context.

THE OTHER SIDE

From the pools of our inveterate moments
we pull memories
of desperation and inspiration.
How do we know,
when we walk through history's door,
what it is that we are seeing?
How is it that we must remember
there is that "other side"?
Of the many broken pieces of life's mirror,
how often are we given to know:
Good vs. Evil.
Benevolence vs. Destruction.
The other hands holding
a suckling child, slitting a throat?
Are these just pieces of an "oriental moment,"
a broken petal, bent feather, torn leaf, blemished fruit?
How dear we hold those still-lifes
– those frozen moments –
when the whole or its parts
catches us and holds us from here to there
forming infinitesimal bridges
over which we pass and in passing say,
"Save us from ourselves!"

TO DREAM THE DREAM

To dream the dream of lustless time
where passion follows a gentle stream's course,
I hunted for a sanctuary
on the edge of forever-wilderness –
because I too
was hounded by the century of my time.

CLUTCHING HANDS

The clutching hands of ignorance cling.
We shrug and toil with freedom's ring.
Then gasp caught fast in ignorance's clasp
by hands rough and splintered, chafed and rasped.
How is it that we choose to stray
when truth reigns throughout the day?
Still, ensconced on pedestals of sloth,
we rend and tear our tattered cloth.
Wandering and wondering from history's fate,
we stand lost in time entranced behind life's gate.
Then,
from courage's wake we leap to catch
a glimpse of clearing skies
as sun's brilliant flash illuminates all our lies
uttered in unison by politician's movements.
Finally, free we fly in new found moments.
No one holds the precious key to souls' doors
when weakened knowledge ravages lives lost to wars,
or when we of freedom's ilk
lay forgotten gifts on altars
bedecked with woven silk.

WE ACT IN WAYS

We act in ways that speak in soul tongues.
From then to the now,
we parse our possibilities
and then we choose
life or death.
We lie to ourselves
in acts of cowardice or valor,
depending upon how we have administered
the truths of our belongings,
the goodness of our souls,
the yesness of our being.
From one to another,
we cannot bypass those who stand beside us
and so it is that Love reigns, with
"Knowledge, Care, Responsibility, and Respect."[1]
And as a coalescence of the cosmic powder
salts our paths,
we wander in an evanescence of amulets
left to tell.
Seeking,
we find ourselves
– again –
and repeat that ancient prayer,
"As it is now, ever shall it be."[2]
Thus we live,
consumed in Celestial Fires.

---

[1] From the *Art of Loving* by Eric Fromm.
[2] Socrates (Dialog of Phaedo) recalled an ancient prayer just before he died, "I recall an ancient prayer: It is as it was in the beginning, now and forever." Somewhere along the way we added, "Amen!"

RAVEN'S DANCE

What exuberance of heart fills nature's bed?
How can we not anthropomorphize it all,
and then question what we do?
Sailing and banking.
Rising and falling.
What mission stirs the ravens' wings,
points them to their purpose?
We reflect –
to what order of the day
do they respond
as they gargle in the wind?

SANDALS – NO MORE![1]

What are they fighting for
a tribe against its neighbor,
the history of their communal memories,
the oppressed against the oppressors?
Land is forever passing to one
and then another.
Now it's Goretex, all high tech,
and then we realize
we aren't tribal enough.
To battle the many-headed hydra –
are the nuances or our time.
Which to sever first?
The challenge is to start.
Stay focused!
Get centered!
Accept the gifts of life
and all they entail.

---

[1] This refers to the fact that some young boys were conscripted in the upheavals of our day for a pair of boots – something their feet had never known. How large? how small? are some of our desires when disparate circumstances prevail?

TO BE ONE – WE MUST BE TWO

A self-cage bars the doors of forever.
It must,
in the end,
be flung wide.
Trust we have to
the sails of ourselves
– and others.
Only then
can we find a way to love.
And yet,
care to see those less than human souls
mired in ideologies of death,
disregarding the fertility of life itself.
They seek only its desecration.
Agony suffers most always
a lack of purpose.
To go beyond
is always found in freedom
bound to nature's holy drift.

EMPTY TREE

Empty hands of waving branches clasped.
Their layered litter curled in the curtain
of the fall.
All other players lately lilted were too late
for reaping's efforts.
Tombs closed their mighty doors.

IDIOMATIC RELEVANCE

¡Apurate! Sin prisa.[1]
"Hurry up! Take your time!"
Templates of the ages present,
and we wonder and we wander.
What is our Holy Purpose?
The great "Why?" of our existence
shadows and haunts.
We are motivated to question,
always through the pace
of our day …
What does that word that I think I see in my mind,
or hear in my ear,
really mean?

---

[1] "Hurry! But, take your time." There is wisdom from the streets of cultural interface. This is a saying that appeared shortly after NAFTA (the North American Free Trade Agreement) went into effect and U.S. factories were locating in the border zone between the United States and Mexico. We all live on borders.

NECESSARY THINGS[1]

Life is:
a startling woman to love,
children who grow into "Real People,"
grandchildren that astonish,
capable friends.
Then,
and along with,
a passionate commitment to add to the
conversation of our Holy Purpose:
To do something!
That is all!
It is always enough!

---

[1] Self, mate, family, work, and friends are the five cards in *The Game of Life – A Player's Manual for Executives and Others.*

HANDS ON!

Do it now!
Touch!
Caress!
Listen!
Living with the Word turned flesh
is an absolute.
If there is a living dialog,
we are touching.
Admonitions:
Those lost in the existential smoke and mirrors
of our current confusion,
those panting and out of breath,
they must stop and take the extended
hand of truth.
There is an ocean of difference between
healthy skepticism
and the deception of paranoia.
Hold fast!

PINHEADS

They glance into
the cracked mirror
of the Divine
and see only pieces
of an insipid smoky reflection
and think they have a clear path
to become a neo-con or a neo-fascist,
thinking in their tortured eclecticity,
they are on the right path.
Not hardly!

THE MASSES

The masses,
in their current state of stupor
or pseudo-sophistication,
are aware of their ignorance
and they seek justification
by reaching down and wallowing
in the coarseness of the human potential.
Wrapped in a pseudo-pride,
they are driven to wantonness,
to belong.
At whatever level they choose to sink,
they are on a staircase
that only spirals downward.

AWE STRUCK

Imago Dei!
Always beyond,
more than,
forever yet to come,
hinting in the present,
touching the ephemeral.
The pursuit of one,
truth, beauty, justice
is Holiness in the abstract.
The embodiment of
faith, hope, and love
are expressions of
the Infinite and the Eternal.
We wait in joyful hope
for the coming of our savior
Jesus Christ, our Lord.

BEHELD

An osprey whispering by –
breakfast in its talons.

IT HAS BEEN SAID

It has been said
"I come to you from fallen timber,"[1]
born again for the first time.
So who am I
a wandering ephemeral "ought"
that seeks a definition of my being
from some crumbling cultural template
instead of a far distant aurora borealis
of the space/time heavens?
I am an I am,
a conglomerate of being,
a thought-thing with sentience.
I feel season's thrusts and drags,
love another,
covet amulets of history,
know touch, listen and taste.
What ideology drives my druthers?
Must I kill another to be myself?
Only if – means yes.
Whose value mine or yours?
What madness takes us
towards our judgments of others?
Must our life be some rabid frenzy of slogans
saying nothing,
when we all live in that sacred crucible
of shared being
emanating from the heart of One?

---

[1] From "Secret Places," in *Reflections from Lucerne: A Collection.*

MESSIANIC HUBRIS

An exuberant messianic hubris
reigns throughout the politics of the day.
How long will it be
before enough say,
"That's enough!"?

A VISION

What is a vision of freedom worth?
A fighting will that says,
"Remember the known unknown
and the unknown known."
One cannot be half-assed about the rule of law:
The spirit and the letter
is never enough without the mind and heart.

TO MOTIVATE A FEW

Shame is a deeply felt sentiment –
carried in the recesses of our souls.
Yet there are times,
when in danger of losing ourselves,
we reach a catharsis,
and a few summon sufficient courage
to embrace a remnant of their
vestigial honor –
that glorious reciprocal of shame.
And then,
in a supreme sacrifice of our pseudo-selves,
we heroically stand for what we know is right.
Resurrected from the ashbin of our lives,
we choose to grasp that last thread
tying us to our souls.
We choose to embrace the truth
and in so doing set our souls free.
How many will there be who will –
when reaching the precipice of time's squanderings –
turn, stand, remember, and say,
"Now is the time for all good souls
to come to the aid of their country!"
Yet,
still we see hanging from time's lattice
tattered sacred documents
wrought with blood and treasure.
We have left unaided history's greatest gift,
when a few great souls pledged
their lives and sacred honor
to set a world free enough
to continue marching on.

CHEATING TIME

Cheating time.
Memories swirl.
I bask in love of the Divine.

GIFTS

Trees grow in the forests
of Bosnia and Croatia.
Years pass and the lives of people go on.
Causes and counter-causes
blow across the centuries.
Fathers awaiting sons,
mothers mourning daughters
carry silent painful burdens
of those who were never
seen or heard from again.
Just disappeared and gone forever.
Roots of trees seeking sustenance
pass through buried corpses
as waving fronds of pine send
dappling shadows over flowers
left to tell.

LOST AND FOUND

We are the unbounded bounded.
And yet each of us must remember:
If "Where it was – there I am"[1] is true,
I can only re-mind
myself of myself.
"Spurs and sabers
- hang them on the walls of time.
There is restlessness in our souls.
Stand ready!
Be still!
Stay awake!
Pay attention or die!

---

[1] I discovered this in Jonathan Lear's *Love and its place in nature*. However, whether in Sophocles, Freud, Goethe, or anyone in between, or after, I do not know.

OUR TIME

In a fear-driven frenzy we rush and rush
desperately seeking confirmation
of acquired half-truths,
half-truths that would matter
if we only knew which half it was
that indeed mirrored the everlasting:
The will of God,
is this one's fate,
that one's cross,
another's luck.
It is always a yes or a no,
always the full mosaic that is His.
We write and walk the paths
of our times.
An age is upon us –
the coalescence of our kind.
From every corner, every stripe,
festooned with the cultural baggage
of yesterday we come.
From tribal to the insipid secular elite,
the ingredients boil
in the urban melting pots of today.
The currents of time's river
crash over rocks,
passing through placid meadows
and swirling in eddies,
always remaining the same river.

SELF-RESPECT

Self-respect
is that coincidental commitment
to a recognition of who we really are.
Deep down inside us there is,
and for all we know has always been,
a sense of perfecting from which there is no escape
– no alternative to becoming
other than
who we already are.

THE AXE STRIKES THE TREE

From memory's hall
come the crisp sounds of accomplishment.
In them we find a staccato rhythm reminding
of whence came ephemeral heart strings,
tugging dreams, wispy feelings,
all entangling current desires.
Yesteryear's sustenance
bathes tattered senses.
Breathing slows.
A sense of right emerges.
Long forgotten visions flare
in the mind's eye.
Old goals ignite
again those hidden trails
seen so clearly in our youth,
those that could have led us to our soul's haven.
Let my axe strike again that tree.

YES AND NO

I can stand naked in the wind and say,
Yes! and No! to Satan.
Yes! to an existence.
No! to its allures.
I can also choose to say to God,
Yes! Yes! And yes again!
Yes to an existential choice.
Yes to self-ownership.
And yes to a complementing presence.

OBUNTU[1]

The essence of humanity
is the compassion of our kind.
Why do soul-centers often wander in ambiguous
and less than real states of being?
The hail of circumstance cautions our resolve,
and duty to "the other"
emerges as that social tenet
bound to honor history.
Yet there is no honor
that does not give freedom its reigns.
To sound the blessed note that came before
and struggled through its nows
to this edge of eternity,
that's the dream
– beyond conventions –
driven by those soul-winds that build and ravage,
always build and ravage screaming,
"How many truths are there?"
The only answer heard blowing through the winds
of the eternal and caught now in the trumpets
of my ears is,
"Yes!"

---

[1] According to Wikipedia, Obuntu (Ubuntu) is an Nguni Bantu term roughly translating to "human kindness," or human-ness. It is often translated as "humanity towards others," but can be used in a more philosophical sense to mean "the belief in a universal bond of sharing that connects all humanity."

HISTORY

History is a capricious lover
– too long – too short –
always coming, staying late.
When the wise are obliterated
with *sturm und drang*
and the voices of wisdom not heeded,
the innocent perish
until there is a new silent-time
in which we gain sufficient understanding
of our mistakes.
Then it is
that we set ourselves on a new course
toward what we think we finally,
really know.
It is then that the tidbits
of our love affairs with errant ideologies
– those scattered skeletons of the ages –
show their colors.
How soon the bugle's call?
When the lowering of the flag?
Life is always a dance
swaying this way and that,
always on a path
between too much and too little.

THE LAST CONFLAGRATION
(The Abandoned Hearth)

Which small piece is ready for tinder's spark?
What has waited through its drying time?
What dreams were awash in the soft winds of summer
as moisture was pulled
from split oak, maple, and birch,
flaming into creatures of the night,
flickering into sight,
dancing in their throes,
cascading into the coals' embrace?
Wavering tongues
sent signals to pensive eyes
and stalwart hearts of the firewatchers.
What thoughts were stacked on memory's shelves
birthing passion's visions of new desires?
How could it come to pass,
that the fire would be shut behind an iron door,
hidden from sight –
lost to the imagination?
Now kindled flames are locked away,
replaced in a dark chamber of some furnace,
where regulated oil and gas
roar in rigid monochromatic colors
that only hint at tales of lore and times a'back.
History's distillations of our efforts
are forever lost to hearts and minds.
Where will our souls and the souls of our children go
to see, feel, and hear the tongues of fire?

CHOICES

As Allah, blessed be His name, cradles
each warrior's soul,
the opportunities of freedom
present themselves:
to follow the road into heaven
or to leap into the fires of hell.
Where are the hues and cries of the Mullahs
and the Imams exhorting and admonishing
wayward souls?
It is not with courage that the devout
hold their tongues in fearful witness
of the slaughter of innocents.
To hunch their backs in prayerful silent hubris
blackens every soul so inclined.

ON MY WAY AGAIN!

May I awake to the quadrants of my space
(a square with the corners connected,
each to its opposite)
and to the "books of my forevers"
– and on my way again –
to the woodshed of my dreams,
to the feeding of the livestock,
and the tending of the garden of my necessities,
to the office of my creations,
to the labyrinth of illusions,
and finally,
to return to the depths of my slumbers.
Then –
to rise again,
and upon occasions,
to hunt the Sojourner's Path
directly to my creations
from whence I cross over to my illusions
and there
choose brief reveries of passion
seeking again my woodshed,
hardly remembering at all
the crystal goblet of my centered self
hanging in the vortex of my path.
I wander wondering through my days.

THE VOICE OF THE PEOPLE

The voice of the people
always arises from the lips of the past,
is always a part of the lives of others.
The vagaries of individuals and cultures in their pasts,
beyond their pasts,
perturbed in presents too removed from futures,
always gives birth to a common voice.
Contained in that élan of yeses,
when hand, heart, and deed
gave birth to the life of another,
sharing a continuation of our kind,
there was established a voice of the people.
Now,
in the insipidness of a superimposed
politically correct silence,
how can the creature of the 21st century
continue to cultivate
a culture of imagination
that feeds the personal and communal
– perpetuating the freedom of our kind?
When anything happens,
it is always to position one's self in conflict,
construct, fabricate, destroy,
to connect this moment in history.
In the great confluence of the vortices
of the universe,
we must hold the present still
– if only for a moment –
and remember:

In the stillness of the forest
the regal elk steps into view,
the basking trout hides beneath the sunken log.
Cut the innocuous chatter
– don't befoul the mystery –
it all comes from the hand of God.
From the soft rhythm of the seasons
come the storms of the day.
Snow does not usually fall in July.
Flowing from morning through noon to evening
we must live seeking a pace for us
that matches most of God's moments.
To stop the rushing
– the frenetic movement –
the "on the way syndrome,"
hunt answers to simple questions:
Where am I going?
How will I get there?
What am I going there for?
All surrounded by the omnipresent:
"When?"
Choose Now!
to hearken to the voice of the people.

THE QUESTION

Am I writing of some reverberating echo
in some remote and forgotten canyon,
or am I hinting of some
praise due our Lord?

A STATEMENT OF FACT

What creature are we
in a universe that is and isn't?
We can choose to stand on that staircase of history,
that perspective that binds us to our past,
and yet
what sets us free to coincide with truth itself?
What zigzagged path winds its way
through days and nights?
What postmodern quandary
hangs around our neck?
Hill and vale beckon, and lay foreboding.
Yet we push on.
What would we be if we chose to be
someone different,
not an other and not a self
but a real one?
We feel we must try to choose
and then,
when we move on we will be able to say,
"We're almost there!"
I didn't get here by walking from the library
to the classroom.
I walked from homicide to suicide,
with the mundane and heroic
in between.

A VAST PANORAMA

The serenity of nature's backdrop
confronts the dissonance of the present –
the leavings of a species' footprint.
In the face of the full range of the human saga –
from despair to hope, love to hate,
we now lose life's miracles.
The full spectrum is distracted by everything –
all of the time.
Black on black,
red on red, yellow on yellow,
white on white,
rich on poor.
New walls hem us in
with fractured reflections of cacophony.
Yet,
"Those Far Horizons"[1] still stir our souls,
wonder pulls, pushes, pulsates.
We still choose to survive.
Why are we so incredibly lucky
to stumble upon words that
snag, catch, tear at our souls,
take us to great heights,
throw us into vales,
and lead us on?

---

[1] "Toward Those Far Horizons," in *Iris and Other Things: A Collection.*

41

A MODERN DISEASE

A sickness of our time
is to think that there is so little magnificence.
Life,
as seen through the prism called "news,"
presents so little.
Technological presentations
of a stilted world view abound.
We, you and I,
are here now
surrounded by it all
and we must know much of it is real.
Yet,
I must speak again of the "Other"
so that we can "hold fast"
to it all.

ANOTHER REALIZATION

I am pulled from the edges
and passed through a vortex.
Where does one stand in the whirlpool of life?
From this slurry of movement,
do I seek my peace only in death?
I think not.
Swamps, and sunsets, and moon rises
work for me!

SCRATCHINGS

A pencil's sharpened point
tears the paper
as frenzied furied words bubble and tumble
down the page.
Rage from a torn and bleeding heart
hangs tight around the scuffing sounds
of graphite.
In venting passion's throes,
when sights and sounds of piteous cries
reach raw ears and itching eyes,
it pauses.
Then,
hellhounds steal again the future's hope.
The land is bathed in red.
Feral searches rend dawn's vale.
My day meets your night.
What tumultuous times filled your day
as I slept in oblivion's arms?
Peace is shattered when we finally choose
to own the "goings on"
of "the other side."
Organic metaphors describe
diurnal fluctuations of economics'
stumbling pace.
Futile attempts to match
the 24/7 of the beating heart's
ecstasies and sorrows fail.
Another dawn slashes across still horizons.
And I,
caught in mid-sentence,
scratch on.

AN AGE UPON US

There is upon us a new age,
an age of great transparency of information,
information that births knowledge.
There has always been a lag-time
between those two fraternal moments,
information and knowledge.
This time around there is an inherent attribute
of the one, that births the other.
Never have so many had so much to say.
For the first time in the history of the species,
any person who has a question
(and knows a person who knows another
who has access to the internet)
can type it into a search engine and
(most of the time)
get an answer.
Great fields of common knowledge
and fields on the fringes of the mainstream
are right there at our fingertips.
Romantic poets wrote much about
the reciprocity of touch.
It is now possible to touch
the Noosphere[1]
and to be touched back.

The question now is:
"Have we learned
to be gentle enough, strong enough,
wise enough
to recognize the beauty of life?"

---

[1] The Noosphere – literally, "mind sphere" or Earth's mental sheathe – is a word and concept jointly coined by Édouard Le Roy, French philosopher and student of Henri Bergson, Jesuit paleontologist PierreTeilhard de Chardin, and Russian geochemist Vladimir Vernadsky, in Paris, 1926. The concept has caught the interest of historians, mathematicians, anthropologists, astrophysicists, philosophers, and theologians. See "To Dream," in this volume, and "Celestial Fire" in *Pebbles on the Shore, A Collection.*

CONUNDRUM

Being a poet is like hanging our underwear
on the line outside in broad daylight.
Dangling and waving in the wind
it says all that we are, were, and aspire to be.
We are somewhat like sea otters,
not too large, not too small,
evolution's interesting gift to itself.
We think we are smart and we may be,
and yet we haven't quite learned
how to manage our affairs.
We count the genome and splice parts.
We peek into space and try to touch the stars.
Along the way,
we try to learn how
to touch others and ourselves.
Religious expressions are peculiar.
Some honor life. Some do not.
We wander and we sit.
We laugh and we cry,
and still many, many try to do.

ASSESSMENT

We are always betting on the come –
the eternal forward.
The capricious maelstroms of history
offer brief report that
God's in charge.
In any case,
little do we note,
until He calls our name,
that we have done such paltry things
as walking by a beggar's plight.

DEATH'S WORDS

What if the sum substance
of your funeral oration was:
He soiled the sheets
and poisoned the soup?

DISCRIMINATION

"We can't discriminate against anyone"
is a statement made by an idiot.
Pornography is anything
that does not complement
the joy and art of recognizing
the beauty and sanctity of human life –
all life.
If it is not in the interest of life,
discriminate against the ravaging effects
of the cancers of humanity!
In our attempt to protect life
and conquer those evil bastards,
profile each and every one
in the best interests
of the species.

ADMONITION

This is the best of all possible worlds.
Start here and make it better.
There is a critical mass of good –
yet a few can create a squeaky wheel.
Stay focused!
Grant little,
if any,
press to idiots.

A WISH

Give me
woodland and meadow,
meadow and woodland,
to raise the crops,
to warm the hearths.
Could I hope to be,
should I hope to be that "common man"
of our estranged Kierkegaard?
I would want to be likened to the
"forgotten one,"
the one who bathes
in the
hallowed
simplicity of eternal truths.

FACTS

The inexorable wheels of justice
turn and turn.
The inevitable eventually rises
to the top of being's pyramid
and points us towards
that brilliant star of truth.
Not as a "fixed thing"
but as luminosity,
the life significance
of the existential moment.

FACT OR FICTION?

From what perch of righteousness
do I sit in judgment of the people of an age?
My time is spent parsing truths
of tattered tales.
I flounder on my path
of stolen thoughts.
From myth and legend –
who knows fact from fiction?

FROM WHENCE THE PROPHETS?

What did the species know
before the Prophets came,
or were they always with us –
just speaking in minor tongues?

IMPASSIONED

I must learn to stay
– at times –
my impassioned hand
as I attempt to share my feelings
of history and current events.
A reasoned hand
mirroring the tranquility
of measured reflection
is what we need.
I have
(am having)
an attack of could have beens
and should have dones.
Be still!

JIHAD

I would love you
if you were a true Jihadist –
one who knows
the struggle
is always against one's self.
I would love you
if you were a Jihadist my brother or my sister –
a follower of the Qurán,
blessed be the Prophet.
He left us with his world and his words:
"Be one!"
The Compassionate.
The Merciful.

LAND

Land is never
"Just a piece of land."
It is the mirror of God's hand
caressing the soul.

POST-IT NOTE

News
"at the speed of live"
means
some isn't.

SELLING THE LAND

The smell of humus,
the girth and stature of trees,
bracken in the shadows,
silent flitting songbirds,
the broken staccato of a woodpecker's bill,
a doe with fawn,
a fleeting glance of a buck,
the long-fingered tracks of a raccoon
in sodden soil,
or the droppings from a porcupine
ensconced in a hemlock,
boughs lying scattered in the snow,
checking the fox den in spring
for signs of kits at play,
pulp piles and Diamond,
the Old Ranger's presence,
a mother's meal,
the first visit of the Lady.
The litany of memories goes on and on and on.
What is the worth of each square inch?
About 2.2 cents.
What price paradise?
Surely, not the value of a soul.

SLEEP

Sleep is when the blackness of within
meets the blackness of without
and I fall into the oblivion of in-between,
losing myself into myself
in the quiescence of His arms.

STILL BLINDED

History's walls are tall.
They comfort us and blind us.
Then,
when we step into a breach,
fear and wonder burst upon another scene
and we feel the need to choose again,
to turn away leaving a single trail
saying no to all others.

A DESCRIPTION OF CONFUSION

What sot of snotty snobbishness,
mired in their lust for power,
stands at the helm of citizenship?
What purpose hints a barnacled sloop
with tattered sails?
What helmsman steers her course?
Who tends her creaking timbers?
Who is captain of the ship of state –
that gnarled-bodied conglomerate
of staunch and wayward souls?
Is she off course, or on?

* * *

Just do what you do well
with love for humankind.
Stay the course of commitment.
Offer assistance to the world
and all those in it.
Shed that messianic mantle!
Seek ageless wisdom –
those simple truths
that speak volumes to us all.
Heed the call of freedom!

WRONG CHOICE

Staring into the face of benevolence each day,
we choose to see the shadows
from whence our fears consume us.

WINNING THE PRIZE

We stand
as a people blessed by history,
by circumstance.
Teilhard de Chardin said
we would create a Noosphere netting the globe,
that we would share our very best
along with
"the negative of the photograph."
Let us not dwell on the one
while forgetting the other.
May our current efforts be a testimony
to our soul's accomplishments.
Stride on!
Make straight the way!

WHAT'S HE DOING?

Give me a good shovel,
preferably in the shade,
to sort the stuff of gardens and foundations,
to level and to heap.
I seek to plant and conquer space.
And if it must be under a searing sun –
let it be!
I have need to purge myself of my misdeeds.
Let each drop of sweat that pores deliver
be a sign seeking forgiveness
of self and others.

WE ARE ALL CHILDREN

In the warrens of the world,
we all seek our cubby holes –
safe silent niches that surround us
and hold us.
We are, after all,
only children wandering
in the vast space/time of the universe.

TRUTH'S LADDER

As the changes from spring to fall
give us births and deaths –
so too the movement of politics rises and falls.
Lines are drawn,
borders and ideologies wiggle from cocoons
and metamorphose,
eventually becoming
the crinkling parchments of history.
We are tempted by fragments to create
grandiose romantic facades,
or realistic slices,
from which we draw
"right" and "wrong" conclusions.
Scurrying rats have abandoned the ship.
"We stayed and upheld our ideals!"
"We left and upheld ours!"
These become the murmured invectives
of lives lost to static visions.
Both are condemned to the ash-heap of history.
Integrate and amalgamate
are the only paths to the future.
Forever "the whole truth" stretches out before us:
Sanctify the present with a loving heart
and swift punishment.

Remember:
The children come as our guests
to the party of life.

THE LIE

The asininity of the lie
is to educate for sustained ignorance.
Education must be that pedestal
upon which truth stands
in all its glory.

TRAGIC/COMEDY

The tragic/comedy of human existence
continues to play out
in the theater of our time:
to live, or to die.
Life,
is the somewhat known tragic/comedy:
Death,
the unknown presumable tragic/comedy.
From whence
the stillness of our beckonings,
predilections,
our longings?

THE IDIOCY OF IT ALL

While affirmations or injunctions
such as
"Allah Akbar!" and "May God be with you!"
are true,
we must constrain our personal hubris
and admit that our ignorance knows no bounds –
His house is large!
His ways are infinite!
God be praised!
Allah the Compassionate the Merciful,
Be Praised!
etc., etc., etc.
The history of the species tells us much.
(Much used respectfully in the Face of the All.)
Blood is red in the species hominid,
whether Sunni, Shia, Texan, or –
oh what the hell –
everyone!
Would that transplanted kufr kidney,
etc., etc., etc.
that fills the void
in a member of the radical Umma
etc., etc., etc.
bring with it,
a predilection for McDonald's, Macy's, Mortgages,
etc., etc., etc.?

If a person stands, kneels, or bows
once, twice, thrice
in the presence of a flower's essence,
does the action depict
a true believer or an apostate?
Trophic responses abound!
If you shoot at me, I will shoot back.
If you smile at me, I will return the grace.
If you offer your hand in friendship,
I will climb aboard.
In the face of the unbounded
beauty of humanity
only idiots get it wrong –
and not always.
What does an idiot do when they are thirsty?
WE ARE ALL THE SAME!
Does the All spend His time laughing,
or crying at our ignorance?

GRAND DESIGN

The forms,
given by the movement of it all,
waver in water's translucence,
then clear upon occasion.
Yet, for the most part,
they still remain opaque
like that bridge from the ideal to the real.
Great moments in history
rise up on the landscape of time
as ponderous peaks scaled with the joys,
tears, passions, commitments,
and the sufferings
of those who've gone before.
Just as deserts and jungles provide
other interludes
in the leavenings of the species' soul.

THE DOUBLE-EDGE SWORD

The sword of truth has two sharp edges.
One slices its way toward the truth of life,
that complementary effort
of life to life.
The other lies in the
madness of the hurried moment,
when patience's presence
is lost to hubris of intellect or soul
in which we forget our purpose
and slice away at innocence
victimizing the children.
Coming from behind
they stumble on the
"other side"
and too many are left to die
in wide-eyed disbelief of wounds
intended and misguided.
Hold fast!
Be not rigid,
lest we desecrate their wonder
and willingness to try
that first word, first step,
always made in joyful hope
for the coming of their freedom,
freedom needing to be guarded and released
into an ever-new and growing
circumstance of change.

Hold with gentle staying
as we step to the heartbeat of our times.
Remember water,
the life-blood of the species,
flows in ripples,
reflecting then obfuscating.
We must wait ready upon the truth of our time.
It is always already there
just beyond our known horizons.
Hold! Hold! Hold!
Hold yourself!
Hold them!
Hold it all!

AGE WEARS

Age wears the stone.
Gentle movements of the seasons
nudge, chip, scrape, abrade
the surface.
All wearing a bit away
until that very last crystalline grain
of quartz
rolls its way downriver
and splits into infinitesimal shards
that dissolve
in the onslaught
of water, light, and time.
A life is gone.
Where is it that soul maintains?

WHAT AM I DOING?

…jostling along through some distorted reflection,
locked now in mirrors of the past,
winding my way in a broken holographic tunnel,
turning here – then there,
as pieces of a mind stumble over a path
leading me on to only God knows where.
There is but one practiced effort
that contributes to brief dawnings of moments
when groping in hope –
I know that I know –
He is here and there with me
and I am still with the I AM.

ALMOST ...[1]

In grief we fight from moment to moment,
never knowing
yesterday's truths or tomorrow's lies.
With blinders on we see only cataracts of time,
falling, falling,
dropping off to God knows where.
I seek to know,
help me in my unknowing.
And finally,
when shall I know that the intellect knows so little?
When from the depths of some abyss
pristine drops of water come,
and touching me
they find and baptize a soul
wanting, wanting
so much to be touched by the truth,
to be free.
How could I know how wonderful it feels
to be a self if it were not for you?
And what do I say
when the gentle breeze calls for a response?
Madness is just madness.
Glory lies to justify the madness.
And yet,
in their souls lies a hidden time
when truth is one.

---

[1] This first appeared in *Sign Posts: A Collection of Essays Volume V.*

DROWNING

When ashes fall into themselves
and rotten ice crystals
crash into the water,
I hear the tinkling
of their disappearance.
It is then that
– I feel –
– almost –
ready to believe
in the beneficence of the Divine.
I try to take that one last step
and realize it isn't mine,
it's His
taking me home.
I breathe,
"Abba, forgive my hubris!
– Please!"

JUST A FEW

Always there are times
when the shadows of the beasts
lurk among the many,
the many who,
with backs bent and eyes on their separate goals,
fail to notice the gathering hoards,
or that single stealthy malevolent one.
And yet,
there are always those other ones,
the purposeful ones,
those few who dedicate themselves,
those few who maintain a watchful eye,
who remember:
"Vigilance Oh Lord! Vigilance Oh God!"
As the masses rush to their chosen pursuits
we must be ever thankful
for those who watch and read the winds of time,
those cataclysmic undertows that
threaten the goodness of us all,
those guardians,
those stalwart,
those timeless,
those ever-vigilant:
those few who fight the good fight,
those few who know their purpose.
Always those few essential ones
who labor in the vineyard for us all.
They keep their lonely vigil.
To those we bow and say,
"Thank you and well done!"

LEFT TO TELL[1]
(And Found!)

They come!
The depth and breadth,
the richness of the texture,
the vastness of the beauty
grabs hold of a perception
flooding the fullness
of the human landscape.
Beyond wow!
Awe spreads and spreads,
rushing into every human endeavor
splashing vibrant color,
with such incredible movement and sound.
The flashes come and come
and present themselves
to my eyes and mind.
I am caught speechless by the wonder
– and that I may be its witness.

---

[1] A scrap of paper from 15 years ago, a snippet and nothing more – until read it reminds.

PAY ATTENTION OR DIE!

From the plethora of the plasticities of the age,
we must shelter ourselves
and immerse ourselves.
And yet,
beware the eclectic dynamic that creates
a pseudo frenzy
disturbing all those
who have not been able to see
the infinitesimal enclaves
available to every seeking soul!
Serenity reigns!
As every coin of truth has two sides:
Nature's omnipresent mandate:
"Pay attention or die!"
illicits, of necessity,
the need for those essential pauses,
the ones that apprehend the sacred stillness
of the now,
letting us "know" the peaceful pathways
of the Divinity's open arms
and gentle voice saying,
"Be still and come to me,
I am always and forever with you."

THE DYING AND THE DEAD

The dying and the dead are all we have.
The dead are gone,
only remnants remain.
The dying,
the rest of us,
seek to play a role of some "other time"
when the dead were living.
Yet we always do our living in a
"new time."
In this existential conflict,
we attempt to sort out the
value/purpose of our lives.
What and for whom do we live?
It cannot be just for us
– an individual "I."
We are already a "given"
– a conglomerate
shoved (or pulled) into a present.
Anaximander's Love/Hate
is the Yes! or No! of ourselves.
To disregard the vagaries
(the sanctity of it all)
of time and circumstance,
we settle on an open and uncompromising
Yes!
It is the only sensible, rational,
soul-homing exercise
for us to do.

THE ORB

The orb,
the within and without
has proven itself to be an eternal
"Within."
We have been looking at the cross
from a perspective of up and out.
It is within:
We and It are one!
From our historical linear standpoint,
we are emerging into a contemplation
of the Eternal Now.
The mystic Pierre Teilhard de Chardin
hinted of our current dilemma:
"Man not as static center of the world
– as had been thought for a long time –
but as axis and arrow of Evolution,
which is much more beautiful."[1]
We are the arrow –
"the head."
We have become.
The Omniscient is.
Finally,
we do not give up the ghost,
we become the ghost.
Amen, Alleluia!
Alleluia! Amen!

---

[1] From *The Phenomenon of Man*, by Pierre Teilhard de Chardin.

THE SOUL SPEAKS

The Rauch,[1]
always the Rauch,
rolling, coiling, sifting, winnowing,
forever casting grains of sand
from the edges of infinite and gigantic dunes.
And then,
roiling once again
across the mainland and the sea,
always the same, always different.
And yet,
in each crucible of time,
in every cauldron,
there is more and more consciousness,
more and more awareness of
ecstasies and sorrows.
To each conscious unit,
to each aware soul,
there is a
"Yes!"
breathed from and to each syllable
of time.

---

[1]Rauch – Hebrew, meaning wind or breath (God). See "Rauch" in *Reflections from Lucerne: A Collection* and "Image and Likeness" in *Pebbles on the Shore*, and also "I Am an I Am!" which first appeared in Volume IV of *Sign Posts: A Collection of Essays*.

DAWN RISES

The dawn rises,
again,
from the depths of nocturnal quiescence
and stretching itself across the sky
raises the heads of the drooping daisies
gracing the fields.
Another day says,
"Yes!"
to the world.
From the darkest shadows of the night
emerges the brilliant colors of the day.

MY FATHER AND MY BROTHER
– AND ALL HIS FRIENDS TOO!

Smoke rising from the "Old Sugar Bush"
at the bottom of the hill.
Spring slush smashed to mud and mush.
Through naked maples,
drenching boughs with remnants of themselves,
sift smoke and steam.
What glorious process,
giving in their growing,
sharing in their flowing,
staying in their dying.
Then split to cord-wood
feeding hearts and hearths.
40 to 1!
that age old formula of sap to syrup.
The Tapper,
the Gatherer,
the Fire-builder,
the measured Pan-filler,
courageous in their every move!
Finally!
the bobbing bulb hails
the perfect moment –
sweet water to amber syrup!
Nostril and taste buds titillate
as memories cascade back
to times ago when waffles and pancakes,
bedecked with blueberry compote
and maple syrup,
all accompanied the eggs, pork links, bacon,
and fried potatoes
becoming food for stomachs
and that sensuous part of our souls.

All renderings of the Native Americans
and their singular efforts
to wrestle from the wilderness
that sucrosed brown crystal.
And it was
– that there he was –
– that younger brother of mine –
dedicated to a purpose and a sharing of the gifts.
Thank yous! Kudos! Applause!
Well done!

SEDONA MOMENT

So ...
when wearied of the onslaught of the centuries,
or yesterday's news,
having been drawn down
in your estimation of the species' efforts ...
stroll through the Hill Side Galleries in Sedona
and imagine the flowing of talented hands and minds that
created all the works of art.
Feast upon the paintings,
touch the sculptures,
and gaze at the red rock cliffs.
After which,
I dare you to be not proud of God's
and others' talent.

TO THE POST-POSTMODERNS

Shatter the circle!
Go through the vortex!
Enter the Black Hole!
Cast aside holographic accretion.
We where?
Going here?
Turn!
Turn!
Gaze in!
Gaze out!
Who?
What?
Touch!
Love!
Now!
Forever!
Nothing more!
The Cruciform's pedestal?
Ah! Yes,
perhaps ...

THE AGE'S WISDOM

Squirrels search in spring
for last year's benevolence.
Could we do less and still survive?

TO THE BASTARDS OF DEAD CREEK

It is rumored:
They convened and connived.
They colluded and contrived.
In those heady days of the Crandon Mine
I believe it was called the DNR
and before that the WCD.[1]
To which would one ascribe a modicum to voracity?
The latter of course!
It bespoke a commitment to conservation,
the former rallies round the political arena.
In their hubris they supposed,
and I still suppose,
that God wasn't watching.
They hid behind a meeting of closed doors.
A "consensus,"
a "fact finding,"
I believe is what it was called.
Which politician's,
and in particular whose name,
was on the order?
That singular document that declared,
"Swamp Creek is a dead creek."
What sanctimony did the idiots possess
when, in secret meetings, they chose to kill a creek?
While it is true that seasons come and go
and ages have their day,
there is an apex to all things.
Eventually we're all overshadowed
by old Father Time.

And yet today ...
when I stood watching
the pristine waters flowing through the culvert
at Keith Siding,
I saw clear water
trickling over moss-covered rocks
and amber-colored sand
heading on its way to Rice Lake,
and beyond.
And perhaps,
in those ever-wondrous caverns of the deep,
to make its way to
the Wolf, the Wisconsin, the mighty Mississippi,
and the sea.
Who could be so wrought
with such a false sense of power and greed
that they would declare,
"Swamp Creek is dead?"
Let's hope no one and forever!
Amen!

---

[1]DNR – Department of Natural Resources, something to be politicized, bartered over, encroached upon, wrangled with. WCD – Wisconsin Conversation Department, something to care about, husband, save, cherish. I think they called the name change progress perhaps a derivative of Progressive – maybe. How close did they come? We may never know.

THE FLOUNDERING FOOTSTEPS OF HISTORY

The floundering footsteps of history
have castrated the mind and confused the soul
– yet we continue to search.
From those great reciprocals
of being's thrusts and drags
– the earth of heaven and the heaven of earth –
we choose again our current plate
where sanctimony is served,
humility reigns,
and the still point beckons.

I CANNOT GO – I CANNOT STAY

I cannot go, I cannot stay.
We have become the "IT" of the All.
I am the modality of self-coincidence
where the awareness of my very being
announces to myself a feeling of
"Why did He make us chalice and goblet?"
The answer comes,
"To nourish one another!"
Premonition:
the vestige of an apparition
and as well the hint of a locution
emanating from and to a locus
announcing myself to myself
and in this awareness I come to know my I,
which shows my me to myself
in that synergism of the audio
(rhythms)
and the visual
(shimmerings)
that catches my, "I am."

EVERY LIFE

Every life – A prayer.
Whispered,
screamed,
spoken,
mumbled,
shouted,
offered.

THE ALL OF HISTORY

It was in the age of implosion.
It was in the age of confusion.
It was in the age of transition.
It was in the age of transformation.
It was in the age of the second great flood.
It was in the age of the great drowning.
It was in the age steeped in information.
It was in the age of disinformation.
It was in the age of the hominid's great loss.
It was in the age of the hominid's great finding.
It was in the age of light.
It was in the age of darkness.
It was in the age of right.
It was in the age of wrong.
It was in the age of the great fruition of relativity.
It was in the age of black holes.
It was in the age of accretion.
It was in the age of the holographic.
It was in the age of the electromagnetic pulse.
It was in the age of entropy.
It was in the age of looking out.
It was in the age of looking in.
It was in the age of joy.
It was in the age of great sadness.
It was in the age of life.
It was in the age of death.
It was in the past.
It was in the future.

And so it was that here now, too,
I am for me.
And yet,
it is that here I am also for you.
For the message says:
"In Him, through Him, by Him"
so that we all may live.
We are Him and He is us.
To know this;
I must know me.
I must know you.
I must know Him.

FLEETING THOUGHTS

Boiling apparitions of the mind
leap from this to that,
from moments of history's groping efforts
to flights of freedom's fancy,
all the while
ignoring the essentials
of personal needs
(not wants)
and the concomitant
personal responsibilities.
If it is truly I who am,
then it must be mine that I must be.
It is I who must give my me to myself.
I cannot wait upon my brother or my sister.
I cannot expect a government to create
a space and time for me.
I must live my life as a sacred gift
from the Giver to myself,
a gift that I can share with any
who so wants to share their own gifts
of personal freedom, creativity,
and responsibility with me.
Stride on!
Oh great heart of mind and soul.
Be all that you can be;
all that you already are.

FOUND

I have found You
along the paths of my forevers.
I have met You
in the perfecting of the seasons,
closings and openings of the day,
waxings and wanings of the flowers,
gurglings of the streams,
falling of the water.
In light and in darkness
You are found.

EXIT STAGE LEFT

Which one,
which thematic moment
will be that last one?
Which facet of the diamond –
which reflective burst of light
from that rippled surface
will catch an eye,
arrest a body,
grab a soul?

* * *

Was it all just a mysterious wind
blowing across the sea of time
or was that shadow,
a touch,
an Immaculate Conception
that gave birth
to a blessed event –
one that set a new stage
for the holiest of stories –
a child was born,
a man to come
– one of us –
come to save us from and for ourselves?
History was changed,
punctuated, brought to a pinnacle
from which a message was cast:
"Love thy neighbor as thyself."
For each and every one,
that is all.
Exit stage left.

* * *

And yet –
we live haunted.
The minutiae of life abounds in
every second,
every minute,
every hour,
every day,
every week,
every month,
every year,
every life.
In all their permutations,
our choices count forever.

ANOTHER QUESTION –
ANOTHER ANSWER

Why am I here if not to witness?
From the wavering luminosity
of life-dancing ripples
on the sandy bottom of a lake,
comes a realization:
I too,
have participated in causing them to be
and to dance.
Again, I utter,
"Amen! Alleluia! Alleluia! Amen!"

A PERSON

A person,
an image and likeness,
presents itself.
What constellation of events
makes a person a person?
Time and space surely play a part –
history wraps its arms around our knowing
(being)
and we are caught in those
tumbling times from which we come.
The events of the ages adhere and dispose.
Myth and legend merge from learned stories
and surge to the forefront
of our selected druthers:
Choices!
Always choices!
Heroically we attempt to justify our beliefs,
beliefs that we employ
to weigh and measure
those choices,
our choices,
choices that have bloodied the earth
maligned our souls,
torn asunder relationships of family,
and of love,
and as well,
inspired our heroics.

* * *

Why is it that in the face of difference
we resort to modes of being
that do not complement
the needs of the human family?

What cursed daemon
sits upon our right shoulder,
what gargoyle perches upon the left?
Why in the face of nature's benevolence
do we insist on wallowing in chaos
when we all stand in wonder and awe
at the birth of a child?
Simple truths befriend us all.
To these we must adhere,
to these
we owe an everlasting thankfulness.
Nature's profound mandate
– Pay attention of die! –
must be met with a
chorus always singing,
"Yes to self! Yes to life!
Yes to *all* life!"

OUR GREATEST LIE

We teach the young to be cynics,
when they should be looking
for a deeper understanding of compassion.
This is our greatest lie.
Yet, it is also done
that when my part slips into the "Whole"
and I know it,
then too,
I know that I am known.
The serenity of it All empties Itself
into me and I into It.
Time stops as It all becomes a yes!
There is no-thing anymore.
It is become –
and in that intensity of "I am!"
I am enveloped in the cloud
of the Known–Unknown.
It is done![1]

---

[1] This is the gift that we should be giving to the young. Shame on us for the lies we have told.

WHOSE NATURE?

Out of the silence in the forest primeval
come the roaring bear
and the howling wolf,
unleashing naked ferocity of life upon life.
Survival reigns supreme!
Tearing pieces of flesh from carcasses
strewn among the ferns and rocks
wary eyes sweep surrounds.
And so ...
urges prevail as people walk the back alleys
of a megalopolis of every continent
seeking satisfactions of depravity
as strains of music and noise,
and the aroma of smoke
float from open doorways and windows,
drifting down causeways.
Such is this thing we call life
in those seldom moments of honest reflection.
How close to the mouth of the cave do we wander?
And why still do we ask,
"From whence springs the softness of seasons
that so inspire
those haunting memories of hope?"

WE PLANT STONES

Amulets of wonder as a child,
bookends as an adult,
a memory of some summer trip,
errant walk in the mountains,
or along stream beds,
fields of stones –
all harbingers of those moments.
We build homes and capitals of stones,
carve edicts of the ages on stones,
names on headstones for loved ones,
and eventually,
for ourselves.
We plant and harvest stones.

FOR ALL THE OLD LOGGERS,
THEIR BRIDES, AND THEIR PROGENY

A RESTING PLACE

This piece is dedicated to Nu-Roc[1] and to all the people who work there caring for each other and their patients.

Jack (John) Tremble looked around the bunkhouse of the logging camp, remembering all the years he had spent moving from one camp to another as opportunity presented and work permitted. He realized that a good number of years were bound up in camps from Swamp Creek, Palmer's, Keith and Hiles, Conner's, and others like Roger's, Flanner-Steger, and Weber's, and then his favorite, McAlpine's, about a half mile back off the shores of beautiful Lake Lucerne. In those seldom moments of reflection, he walked her shores and speculated on its many islands – sanctuaries, he called them. A place where ducks, loons, kingfishers, and those stalwart little shore birds busied themselves running up and down the water's edge, where squirrels spent endless hours playing in the tree branches while keeping a wary eye on the eagles perched in the high branches of the dead snags.

He pictured heaven as a still water moment where life unfolded in its serenity of purpose under the watchful eye of some greater mind, some unknowable, unfathomable spirit that moved and shook the earth, making all things possible. At times he even waxed a bit poetic and wondered in his many notes and scribblings of a Great Divine.

---

[1] See Nu-Roc at the end of this volume.

He recalled moments in McAlpine's camp: there were nineteen bunks and sixteen occupants. Each one was a story, each one a history. Now, crossing over his sixty-seventh year, Jack reflected on his many years of working in the camps back East. How he had started in Pennsylvania and finally, having worked his way up into the old Northwest Territory, a part of which had become several states, Wisconsin being one of them, he was now at his final destination. The hard work and age were catching up with him.

His mind shifted to his life journey, choices, and the moves, reasons he used to keep on moving, never looking back, only thinking of the next job or the next night on the town. He wondered just how many bottles of whiskey he had consumed before his personal epiphany. After which he stopped drinking and began to accumulate a library of sorts, some classics, a few novels, even some articles in the field of physics. He discovered that he had a wide-ranging mind, one that begged to know, to grasp some deeper understanding of the world and the people in it. His predilection for pondering had finally settled on those around him, his fellow loggers. For years now he had continued to read, yet he spent most of his communal hours listening and talking to his fellow loggers.

At long last, having arrived at this particular moment, a time when the logging camps were closing down, the great "logging off" of the north woods was coming to an end. In his reflections he speculated on what would happen to him and the others. Where would they go? What would they do? Who has any need for, or even cares about an old logger?

As his campmates had come and gone they had provided him with a veritable cascade of occupants who shared their stories. He reflected on the significance of each person and their lives. Long ago he had come to realize that there was always a story in each and every pair of eyes, behind each countenance. He enjoyed those touching moments when fellow human beings would share their personal trials, trails, joys, and conundrums. Life itself was a patchwork quilt of times and places encompassing, among other things, one's self-perception, while here and there, tucked between, there was always a hole in those life-blankets of memories and experiences where the cold could creep in and motivate a person to roll over and give up, or get up and move on. And there was always that omnipresent alcohol, which had buried more than a few loggers.

His mind drifted back to his own life. He had been born in Baltimore, Maryland, and was educated at a Catholic school – nuns and all. He remembered them fondly, so dedicated to their task of teaching and worshiping. And yet, there were always those lingering thoughts: What was the rest of their simple lives really like? What did they do on weekends? Where did they go for vacations? It wasn't until he was much older and more seasoned in the understandings of the world that he began to think back and see more of the "whole of things." Some were truly dedicated with an incredible disposition to joy and sharing, really immersed in the task of serving. There were others, however, who were anything but happy.

He left home when he was sixteen to "Go West!" as the saying was. The lore of the "Big Trees" and the "Logging Camps" had grabbed his imagination and given him a goal. He longed to experience "the forests primeval" of that great poet, in Longfellow's illustrious words.[1]

He had always found this knowing/sharing very interesting. One might even say he had dedicated his life to giving a deeper understanding of the dynamics of human life's considerable

---

[1] Longfellow's *Evangeline: A Tale of Acadia*.

effort. The late 1800s and early 1900s, when the last of the Great North Woods were sacrificed to the progress of a nation, was a turn of the century which burst forth with the great understanding that the world was moving toward some grand purpose, some great awakening.

In his later years he spent his spare moments, when he was not working as a sawyer or skidder, engaged in conversations, observations, and reading. He read the Good Book, along with some of the Classics, and whatever current events came his way. He remembered his father spending evenings reading literature in various fields and his mother's admonishment to read: "Read if you want to know," she would say, "Read! You can read a book about anything!" she would add. This and her dedication to household care, and those in it, consumed her years. And so it was that he read, and read, and read. He remembered her as a talker and his father as a silent man.

He reflected on his youth and his schooling days wherein those reflective moments that occurred, moments of deep thought; he felt he had heeded both of their examples to mine the richness of life. He was indeed a blend of both of them.

In the course of events he came to understand that much of what one thought about those short glances at the vagaries of life, or a short shift at this job or that, was not the whole story. In his travels through Pennsylvania, Ohio, Michigan, and finally to northern Wisconsin, working on farms, and in factories, he had come to know that being from a small but loving family was not a universal experience. In moments of "memory-washing" as he called them, moments when he distilled more of what could have been and probably was, as his powers of reasoning and experiences in the folds of life's curtain were exposed to new ideas and the light of reflection, he came to know more of the vastness of the human sea.

Now, as he sat on the edge of his bed, in what was called an "Old Folks Home" and some were even now referring to them as "Nursing Homes," he stared out the window and let his mind wander over the years. He had never married and therefore there were no children to be concerned about their "old man." What good was an old man? That thought had gained some prominence in his mind as the days mounted into years and he became aware of his declining faculties and as he watched the old loggers leave the camps. What did they, the old people, have to offer? It was a daunting task, losing one's physical capabilities and the deep pool of memories and trying to make some sense of it. Had he married he would have had a very different set of circumstances.

Well, he hadn't. The years had slipped by and the few dollars that he was able to accumulate were sent back home to help care for an aging mother. His father had long since passed on. And now, his mother had been gone for some time too. He hadn't given much thought to those declining years and the inevitable ending of one's life. In retrospect, he felt somewhat ashamed that he had not placed a greater value on money. After all, he was a great advocate of the adage, "Nothing Is Free."[1]

He would recall falling a big pine in windy weather, "stealing it from the wind," is what the loggers called it. The tree was never notched to fall into the wind, only at some oblique angle where once it started to move and the weight became a factor, one could lay it down where one wanted it. "To hit the peg," the Jacks called it. And he was, in his own time, one of the best. He smiled, recalling the sense of pride he felt among his fellow loggers. All appreciated those with talent. Either you

---

[1] See "It's Free!" and "Nothing Is Free" in *Sign Posts – Collections of Essays*, in Volumes I and IV respectively.

had it or you didn't. And those who didn't couldn't brag. A logger's life was eminently transparent. Either things went well or they didn't and the proof was there for all to see.

There were always those other moments when you could sit quietly on your bunk and read, converse, or listen to some piece of music on the phonograph or someone singing a chorus or two. Those moments, for him, were special times when he could study the thoughts of the ages or the current thoughts and wonders. Who was James Matlock, really? Who were Gene Finkle, George Renke, Jorg Jorgensen, and all the others? The list was long. He had developed his personal speculations over the many years and had become what some now would refer to as an amateur social scientist. From the many books and conversations, he had garnered many bits of wisdom, personal insights, and points of view on the human condition.

In the confines of his camp moments, amidst the smell of sweat, the cold, the heat, the noises of sleep, the music of the harmonica, the fiddle, the voice in song, or muted conversations, Jack's acuity of presence garnered lessons of the truths of the human spirit, and among those truths a lot of the good and some of the bad.

And so it was that over the years he gathered what he came to call His Rules ... life's rules, really. They were quasi-secular, or what the literati would call the sacred and the mundane. In other words they were just what a person who thinks, says, and does – if they were serious about being who they really were, are, and forever will have been.

From each indomitable spirit he saw, and felt, a driving force encompassing a self-ownership that expressed itself and honored that same self-expression in others – no matter whom they were or where they were from. The only overriding fact to those many life successes was the absolute need for coming from a position of complete integrity. Falsehoods were the death knell for anyone not acquainted with the apparitions of the Lying One.

In his observations he became aware of certain universals – expressed as gemstones of individual and communal understanding, of human well-being. There was an indisputable fact: knowledge of oneself was crucial in harvesting the fruits of life. And, along with that self-knowledge, there had to be an immediate acceptance of time and place. The current understanding of physics mirrored the life-line of the person. How could things be otherwise – when we really come to know who we really are?

Jack called his first rule: **PLAY ONE!** He reasoned that for each and every person there was indeed only one person and that one person of the self was responsible for whatever rational choices one made. This first rule he dedicated to all his fellow lumberjacks, those stalwart harvesters of the Great Woods – those havens of mystery – those fertile expressions of the Divine's creative plan.

From Steg Larson at the Swamp Creek Camp he felt the deep necessity for valuing the silence of one's mind as a person communed with their surrounds. Steg turned poetic when he spoke of the pregnant silence from which the voice of the Creator whispered those rock-bottom truths about oneself and the world at large. There were in those moments a distillation of only a now that encompassed an awareness of, and an ownership of one's life. Each breath inhaled and exhaled into the "forest primeval" melded the person of the self to their own life and to the world.

From this came his second rule: **STAND STILL IN SILENCE! IN ORDER TO SEE, FEEL, AND HEAR THE ETERNAL TRUTHS.**

It was Karl Ott at Conner's Camp that was always wont to say: Das ist ... Alles ist! (That is what it is! Everything just is!) And he went on to explain, in his well-thought-out Germanic way, the age-old truism: All things are either true or not true – mine or not mine. It was indeed true that many things are true and many things are not. The eternal challenge was to sort out the difference. Age and experience were essential ingredients in this sorting-out process.

And the second part was a home run. All things were ultimately either yours or not yours. Own what was yours and don't take things personally. If they were true and yours, they were true and yours. And if they weren't, they weren't – all sound logic that demanded the utmost of self-responsibility.

In these words Jack found his third rule: **TRUE – NOT TRUE, MINE – NOT MINE.**

As the blade of the saw shed the sawdust it also drew out the essence from the great pine, a sweetness that spoke of the sun's distilling seasons, the wind's marauding efforts, the movements of all things, things that needed to be captured and appreciated in their own time, and in their own way.

It was Hans Krinkle from Palmer's Camp that was so fond of saying, "Get it now!" In the words of the social commentaries of the writers of the day, Hans would have been called a rabid existentialist and maybe even a communist, although Jack really didn't think so. Hans was too personable and respectful of the vast array of human freedoms that led to personal satisfactions and accomplishments to turn all things over to some collective. No, it was his pure joy of the moment that he reveled in. "Carpe Diem!" someone had called it and no one said it better and lived it better than Hans.

From this omnipresent and singularly significant fact, Jack coined his fourth rule: **OWN IT NOW!** In reality there was no other time to build one's portfolio, offer one's honest self-portrait.

Then, there was Jimmy Tyler from Roger's Camp. Jimmy was a quiet sort who was forever giving the language of the Jacks a cleansing and offering his admonition: "All things need to be loved in their own way." He delivered his sensitive and profound message is such a way that all the lumbermen who heard it would turn their heads to one another and silently nod in agreement. In that great fraternal brotherhood of the workers of the woods there was a deep appreciation of the word and the meaning of love. There were few who found it, but all nourished a deep desire to experience the essence of life: To have a wife and hold a child. Love was indeed the grand elixir of life – it was not something one could find in a bottle. Too many were lost and left staring at the bottom of an empty glass with nothing to show for their efforts.

Jack was convinced that in that wonderful eternal process of life, it was indeed love that was the measure of everything. The great writers dealt with the subject in all of its nuances, successes, and failures. Every religion extolled its virtues. It was that crowning glory of all human and divine effort. It became Jack's fifth rule: **ACT IN LOVE.** Knowledge, Care, Responsibility, and Respect were its touchstones. There just was no other way for life to be lived and appreciated.

Jack recalled Gene Chance at the Flanner-Steger Camp. Gene's contribution to the wisdom of the day was that all things must grow, must change, and must mature to become all that nature intended for them to be, in their fullness, in what was called "their plenitude." Gene would admonish the younger and the foolish that only in growth would they find true happiness. He would pose his gift of wisdom as a question: "Why don't you grow up?" It was enough to get them thinking that old Gene wouldn't ask a question unless there was some need for an answer. When it was directed at the thoughts, words, and deeds of a person, and the question was always posed in a public setting, it was difficult to escape the facts at hand. It was this concept of the acquisition of a greater truth, a complementary self-awareness of a new understanding, that provided a chance to change a thought, a word, or an action, to a reflection that brought with it an opportunity for change, for growth and maturity that met with a need to do something differently.

And so it was that Jack divined his sixth rule: **DEDICATE YOURSELF TO GROWTH.** All things must grow or die, and although it says in the Good Book, "It is in dying that we are born to eternal life," it is not something that we are all disposed to do right this minute, or at any rate not while we have things still left on our personal agendas. But the rule did indicate that something was needed right now, not only for the one who had to grow and change, but for those around who were placed in some danger when something foolish was in progress. Timber falling was not without its perils. At one time or another it made believers of all of the Jacks and brought home the absolute necessity for a deep sense of responsibility. One could die or be the cause of another's death. The life of a lumberjack was very real and very dangerous.

Jack lifted his eyes to the fading fall sunset and placed his pencil down on his tablet. In his mind he was back at the McAlpine Camp, knowing this would be his last winter's logging operation. He had finished his short compilation of the

Rules. He contemplated the need for everyone to have some guidelines, some precepts, that if followed, would produce a satisfying productive life. He was struck by a thought to add another mandate to his list, and so the seventh rule emerged in his thinking: **FOLLOW ALL THE RULES – A HOLY ENDEAVOR IS ABOUT TO BEGIN.** It wasn't because there were not holy things, ways, places, and people – it was that now there was a path that could be taken if one wanted to grow in awareness and maximize self-fulfillment and become all that one was, indeed, what one was intended to be.

Jack ended his days at Nu-Roc. Days filled with thought and prayer, days of sharing what he had learned with his fellows and others as they spent their last days waiting for their life's rewards.

THE RULES[1]
PLAY ONE!
STAND STILL IN SILENCE! IN ORDER TO SEE, FEEL, AND HEAR THE ETERNAL TRUTHS.
TRUE – NOT TRUE, MINE – NOT MINE.
OWN IT NOW!
ACT IN LOVE.
DEDICATE YOURSELF TO GROWTH.
FOLLOW ALL THE RULES – A HOLY ENDEAVOR IS ABOUT TO BEGIN.

* * *

---

[1] See *The Game of Life – A Player's Manual for Executives and Others.*

Frances Marie MacFarlane Davison, the wife of the Old Ranger, the Old Forester, the Old Logger (Dave Davison), was to become a resident. She graced a near-corner room where those feathered migrants and yearly residents could stop to refresh and replenish themselves on their daily and yearly sojourns. They would sit in the tree just outside her window and chirp her awake in the mornings of those better days when clouds seemed to want to cover the beauty of the day. They brought her great joy and thanksgiving.

It was there, in her own way, that she also shared the Rules (as she knew them) with those who came to help her and to minister to her in those needful times.

NU-ROC[1]

As the old loggers found a welcome in their waning years at Nu-Roc where they were cared for and nurtured in their last Days as they had been nurtured by their mothers (and those other loving souls), the time would come when their numbers would be out-populated by women.[2]

In a home that was built by a logging magnate for himself and his family, eventually (through an interesting set of circumstances) the old loggers themselves and their progeny, along with many others, came to be inhabitants of the mansion – and finally, the wives and children of those old loggers. Nu-Roc has come full circle in its dedication to the practiced art of caring for each and every one of its guests.

Nu-Roc is one of the best small nursing homes in the nation, and is a shining example of Jack's rules. It originated with a sound business plan and with a concomitant philosophy of loving care for "Old Lumberjacks." In its early days the Newton and LaRocque families came together to establish, under the now-astute care of Paul and Craig Newton, and as well the caring and responsible staff, the "Heaven on Earth" for those elderly who need that special tender loving care in those final days.

To the Nu-Roc family: Well done! And to all those who labor incessantly to fulfill the needs of all those mothers, fathers, and other family members of the rest of us who are so far away and so ill prepared to comprehend the contributions and difficulties of the exceptional professional caregivers and attendants: Stay the course! And finally from the bottom of our hearts: Thank you for all you do for your residents and for us!

[1] A very special acknowledgement and thank-you for their industry and help with this story to Paul and Craig Newton as well as Betty Newton and Dolores Uphoff, and a recognition of Doctors Tinsley and Ovitz for their spirit of caring and dedication, along with Mike Monte and Amanda Flannery who both provided information about the logging camps in the surrounding area, and especially to my brother Peter Davison.

[2] In the infinitude of time – as all things come to pass – the feminine manifests itself in its full splendor and glory. See *The Eternal Feminine*, by Teilhard de Chardin.

www.ingramcontent.com/pod-product-compliance
Lightning Source LLC
Chambersburg PA
CBHW051808040426
42446CB00007B/567